# Receiving Healing from the Courts of Heaven

## Leader's Guide

# DESTINY IMAGE BOOKS BY ROBERT HENDERSON

*Accessing the Courts of Heaven*

*Operating in the Courts of Heaven*

*Unlocking Destinies from the Courts of Heaven*

# Receiving Healing from the Courts of Heaven

## Leader's Guide

## Robert Henderson

© Copyright 2018–Robert Henderson

All rights reserved. This book is protected by the copyright laws of the United States of America. This book may not be copied or reprinted for commercial gain or profit. The use of short quotations or occasional page copying for personal or group study is permitted and encouraged. Permission will be granted upon request. Unless otherwise identified, Scripture quotations are taken from the New King James Version. Copyright © 1982 by Thomas Nelson, Inc. Used by permission. All emphasis within Scripture quotations is the author's own. Please note that Destiny Image's publishing style capitalizes certain pronouns in Scripture that refer to the Father, Son, and Holy Spirit, and may differ from some publishers' styles.

Leader's Guide prepared by Enliven Media

DESTINY IMAGE® PUBLISHERS, INC.

P.O. Box 310, Shippensburg, PA 17257-0310

*"Promoting Inspired Lives."*

This book and all other Destiny Image and Destiny Image Fiction books are available at Christian bookstores and distributors worldwide.

Cover design by Eileen Rockwell

Interior design by Terry Clifton

For more information on foreign distributors, call 717-532-3040.

Reach us on the Internet: www.destinyimage.com.

ISBN 13 TP: 978-0-7684-1760-9

ebook ISBN: 978-0-7684-4474-2

For Worldwide Distribution.

1 2 3 4 5 6 7 8 / 22 21 20 19 18

# CONTENTS

Hello ................................................................. 1

Basic Leader Guidelines ............................................... 3

Steps to Launching a *Receiving Healing from the Courts of Heaven* Group or Class ................................................................. 7

Leader Checklist ..................................................... 11

Session Discussion Questions:
Weekly Overview of Meetings/Group Sessions ........................... 13

| | | |
|---|---|---|
| Week 1 | Healing in the Heavens ............................... | 17 |
| | *Video Listening Guide* ............................... | 19 |
| Week 2 | The Legal Basis for Healing ........................... | 25 |
| | *Video Listening Guide* ............................... | 27 |
| Week 3 | Undoing Trades ....................................... | 33 |
| | *Video Listening Guide* ............................... | 35 |
| Week 4 | The Covenant in Trades ............................... | 41 |
| | *Video Listening Guide* ............................... | 43 |
| Week 5 | Dealing with Dedications ............................. | 49 |
| | *Video Listening Guide* ............................... | 51 |
| Week 6 | The Power of Unforgiveness ........................... | 57 |
| | *Video Listening Guide* ............................... | 59 |
| Week 7 | Undoing Word Curses .................................. | 65 |
| | *Video Listening Guide* ............................... | 67 |

# HELLO!

Thank you so much for joining me in leading my new curriculum, *Receiving Healing in the Courts of Heaven*. As someone who is passionate about ministering healing in others' lives, I'm also excited to equip leaders to do the same thing. It's my hope that as you lead your group in understanding the depths of God's healing, you will experience healing as well.

Over the course of the next seven weeks, you will equip your group as they learn about how the enemy can work legally against them and, more importantly, how to take hold of the gift of freedom God has for them. We are praying for you along the way, that you'd be newly inspired by and armed with the truth of who God is and what He's done!

Thank you again for choosing to lead a group to the Courts of Heaven. Hope and healing await you!

Blessings,

Robert Henderson

# BASIC LEADER GUIDELINES

This study is designed to help you develop into a believer who can cultivate and carry the revelation of the healing power of God wherever you go. From *this* perspective, you will partner with God to see impossibilities bow at Jesus' name and step into the destiny God has for you!

There are several different ways that you can engage this study. These are the standard outlets recommended to facilitate this curriculum. We encourage you to seek the Lord's direction, be creative, and prepare for supernatural transformation in your Christian life.

When all is said and done, this curriculum is unique in that the end goal is *not* information—it is transformation. The sessions are intentionally sequenced to take every believer on a journey from information, to revelation, to transformation. Participants will receive a greater understanding of what partnership with Heaven looks like and learn how enter the courts of Heaven on a daily basis.

Here are some of the ways you can use the curriculum:

## 1. CHURCH SMALL GROUP

Often, churches feature a variety of different small group opportunities per season in terms of books, curriculum resources, and Bible studies. *Receiving Healing from the Courts of Heaven* would be included among the offering of titles for whatever season you are launching for the small group program.

It is recommended that you have at least four to five people to make up a small group and a maximum of twelve.

For a small group setting, here are the essentials:

- *Meeting place*: Either the leader's home or a space provided by the church.
- *Appropriate technology*: A DVD player attached to a TV that is large enough for all of the group members to see (and loud enough for everyone to hear).
- *Leader/Facilitator*: This person will often be the host, if the small group is being conducted at someone's home; but it can also be a team (husband/wife, two church leaders, etc.). The leader(s) will direct the session from beginning to end, from sending reminder e-mails to participating group members about the meetings, to closing out the sessions in prayer and dismissing everyone. A detailed description of what the group meetings should look like will follow in the pages to come.

## *Sample Schedule for Home Group Meeting (for a 7:00 P.M. Meeting)*

- Before arrival: Ensure that refreshments are ready by 6:15 P.M. If they need to be refrigerated, ensure they are preserved appropriately until 15 minutes prior to the official meeting time.
- 6:15 P.M.: Leaders arrive at meeting home or facility.
- 6:15–6:25 P.M.: Connect with hosts, co-hosts, and/or co-leaders to review the evening's program.
- 6:25–6:35 P.M.: Pray with hosts, co-hosts, and/or co-leaders for the evening's events. Here are some sample prayer directives:
  - For the Holy Spirit to move and minister freely.
  - For the teaching to connect with and transform all who hear it.
  - For dialogue and conversation that edifies and is transparent among the group members.

- For the Presence of God to manifest through testimonies and answered prayers.
- For increased hunger for God's Presence and power.

- 6:35–6:45: Ensure technology is functioning properly!
  - Test the DVDs featuring the teaching sessions, making sure they are set up to the appropriate session.
  - If you are doing praise and worship, ensure that either the MP3 player or CD player is functional, set at an appropriate volume and that lyrics are available for everyone to sing along.
- 6:45–7:00 P.M.: Welcome and greeting guests.
- 7:00–7:10 P.M.: Fellowship, community, and refreshments.
- 7:10–7:30 P.M.: Introductory prayer and worship.
- 7:30–7:40 P.M.: Ministry and prayer time.
- 7:40–8:00 P.M.: Watch DVD session.
- 8:00–8:20 P.M.: Discuss DVD session.
- 8:20–8:35 P.M.: Activation time.
- 8:35–8:40 P.M.: Closing prayer and dismiss.

This sample schedule is *not* intended to lock you into a formula. It is simply provided as a template to help you get started. Our hope is that you customize it according to the unique needs of your group and sensitively navigate the activity of the Holy Spirit as He uses these sessions to supernaturally transform the lives of every person participating in the study.

## 2. SMALL GROUP | CHURCH-WIDE CAMPAIGN

This would be the decision of the pastor or senior leadership of the church. In this model, the entire church would go through *Receiving Healing from the Courts of Heaven* in both the main services and ancillary small groups/life classes.

The pastor's weekend sermon would be based on the principles in *Receiving Healing from the Courts of Heaven*, and the Sunday school classes/life classes and/or small groups would also follow the *Receiving Healing from the Courts of Heaven* curriculum format.

## 3. CHURCH CLASS | MID-WEEK CLASS | SUNDAY SCHOOL CURRICULUM

Churches of all sizes offer a variety of classes to develop members into more effective disciples of Jesus and agents of transformation in their spheres of influence.

*Receiving Healing from the Courts of Heaven* would be an invaluable addition to a church's class offering. Typically, churches offer a variety of topical classes targeted at men's needs, women's needs, marriage, family, finances, and various areas of Bible study.

## 4. INDIVIDUAL STUDY

While the curriculum is designed for use in a group setting, it also works as a tool that can equip anyone who is looking to strengthen his or her spirit and soul.

# Steps to Launching a *Receiving Healing from the Courts of Heaven* Group or Class

## PREPARE WITH PRAYER!

*Pray!* If you are a **church leader**, prayerfully consider how *Receiving Healing from the Courts of Heaven* could impact the culture and climate of your church community! Spend some time with the Holy Spirit, asking Him to give you vision for what this unique study will do for your church, and, ultimately, how a Kingdom-minded people will transform your city and region.

If you are a **group leader** or **class facilitator**, pray that those who will be attending your group will be positioning their lives to be transformed by the *knowledge* and *ability* to enter the Courts in this study.

# PREPARE PRACTICALLY!

**Determine how you will be using the *Receiving Healing from the Courts of Heaven* curriculum.**

Identify which of the following formats you will be using the curriculum in:

- Church-sponsored small group study
- Church-wide campaign
- Church class (Wednesday night, Sunday morning, etc.)
- Individual study

## *Determine a meeting location and ensure availability of appropriate equipment.*

Keep in mind the number of people who may attend. You will also need AV (audio-visual) equipment. The more comfortable the setting, the more people will enjoy being there, and will spend more time ministering to each other!

A word of caution here: the larger the group, the greater the need for co-leaders or assistants. The ideal small group size is difficult to judge; however, once you get more than 10 to 12 people, it becomes difficult for each member to feel "heard." If your group is larger than 12 people, consider either having two or more small group discussion leaders or "multiplying" the larger group into two smaller ones.

## *Determine the format for your meetings.*

The Presence of the Lord, which brings transformation, is cradled and stewarded well in the midst of organization. Structure should never replace spontaneity; on the contrary, having a plan and determining what type of format your meetings will take, enables you to flow with the Holy Spirit and minister more effectively.

## *Set a schedule for your meetings.*

Once you have established the format for your meetings, set a schedule for your meetings. Some groups like to have a time of fellowship or socializing (either before or after the meeting begins) where light refreshments are offered. Some groups will want to incorporate times of worship and personal ministry into the small group or class. This is highly recommended for *Receiving Healing from the Courts of Heaven*, as the study is designed to be founded upon equipping and activating believers through encountering God's Presence. The video portion and discussion questions are intended to instruct believers, while the worship, times of ministry, group interaction, prayer time, and activation elements are purposed to engage them to live out what they just learned.

## *Establish a start date along with a weekly meeting day and time.*

This seven-week curriculum should be followed consistently and consecutively. Be mindful of the fact that while there are seven weeks of material, most groups will want to meet one last time after completing the last week to celebrate, or designate their first meeting as a time to get to know each other and "break the ice." This is very normal and should be encouraged to continue the community momentum that the small-group experience initiates. Typically, after the final session is completed, groups will often engage in a social activity—either going out to dinner together, seeing a movie, or something of the like.

Look far enough ahead on the calendar to account for anything that might interfere. Choose a day that works well for the members of your group.

## *Advertise!*

Getting the word out in multiple ways is most effective. Print out flyers, post a sign-up sheet, make an announcement in church services or group meetings, send out weekly e-mails and text messages, set up your own blog or website, or post the event on the social media avenue you and your group use most (Facebook, Twitter, etc.). A personal invitation or phone call is a great way to reach those who might need that little bit of extra encouragement to get involved.

## *Gather your materials.*

Each leader will need the *Receiving Healing from the Courts of Heaven* Leader's Kit, as well as the *Receiving Healing from the Courts of Heaven* book.

Additionally, each participant will need a personal copy of the *Receiving Healing from the Courts of Heaven* workbook. It is recommended they also purchase the *Receiving Healing from the Courts of Heaven* book for further enrichment and as a resource to complement their daily readings. However, they are able to engage in the exercises and participate in the group discussion apart from reading the book.

We have found it best for the materials to all be purchased at one time—many booksellers and distributors offer discounts on multiple orders, and you are assured that each member will have their materials from the beginning of the course.

## STEP FORWARD!

Arrive at your meeting in *plenty* of time to prepare. Name tags are a great idea, at least for the first couple of meetings. Icebreaker and introduction activities are also a good idea for the first meeting.

Pray for your members. As much as possible, make yourself available to them. Embrace the journey that you and your fellow members are embarking on; transformation begins within *you*!

## THANK YOU

Thank you for embarking on a journey to equip the body of Christ to be empowered to know their authority in the Courts of Heaven and bring revival in their lives and communities.

# LEADER CHECKLIST

## ONE TO TWO MONTHS PRIOR

_____    Have you determined a start date for your class or small group?

_____    Have you determined the format, meeting day and time, and weekly meeting schedule?

_____    Have you selected a meeting location (making sure you have adequate space and AV equipment available)?

_____    Have you advertised? Do you have a sign-up sheet to ensure you order enough materials?

## THREE WEEKS TO ONE MONTH PRIOR

_____ Have you ordered materials? You will need a copy of *Receiving Healing from the Courts of Heaven* Leader's Kit, along with copies of the workbook and book for each participant.

_____ Have you organized your meeting schedule/format?

## ONE TO TWO WEEKS PRIOR

_____ Have you received all your materials?

_____ Have you reviewed the DVDs and your Leader's Kit to familiarize yourself with the material and to ensure everything is in order?

_____ Have you planned and organized the refreshments, if you are planning to provide them? Some leaders will handle this themselves, and some find it easier to allow participants to sign up to provide refreshments.

_____ Have you advertised and promoted? This includes sending out e-mails to all participants, setting up a Facebook group, promotion in the church bulletin, etc.

_____ Have you appointed co-leaders to assist you with the various portions of the group/class?

## FIRST MEETING DAY

_____ Plan to arrive *early!* Give yourself extra time to set up the meeting space, double check all AV equipment, and organize your materials. It might be helpful to ask participants to arrive 15 minutes early for the first meeting to allow for distribution of materials and any icebreaker activity you might have planned.

# Session Discussion Questions:
# WEEKLY OVERVIEW OF MEETINGS/GROUP SESSIONS

Here are some instructions on how to use each of the weekly Discussion Question guides.

## WELCOME AND FELLOWSHIP TIME
### *(10–15 Minutes)*

This usually begins five to ten minutes prior to the designated meeting time and typically continues up until ten minutes after the official starting time. Community is important. One of the issues in many small group/class environments is the lack of connectivity among the people.

**Welcome:** Greet everyone as they walk in. If it is a small group environment, as the host or leader, be intentional about connecting with each person as they enter the meeting space. If it is a church class environment, it is still recommended that the leader connect with each participant.

**Refreshments and materials:** In the small group, you can serve refreshments and facilitate fellowship between group members. In a class setting, talk with the attendees and ensure that they purchase all of their necessary materials (workbook and optional copy of *Receiving*

*Healing from the Courts of Heaven*). Ideally, the small group members will have received all of their resources prior to Week 1, but if not, ensure that the materials are present at the meeting and available for group members to pick up or purchase.

**Pray!** Open every session in prayer, specifically addressing the topic that you will be covering in the upcoming meeting time. Invite the Presence of the Holy Spirit to come, move among the group members, and stir greater hunger in each participant to experience *more* of God's glory in their lives.

## INTRODUCTIONS
### *(10 Minutes – First Class Only)*

**Introduce yourself** and allow each participant to briefly introduce him/herself. This should work fine for both small group and class environments. In a small group, you can go around the room and have each person introduce himself/herself one at a time. In a classroom setting, establish some type of flow and then have each person give a quick introduction (name, interesting fact, etc.).

**Discuss** the schedule for the meetings. Provide participants an overview of what the next eight weeks will look like. If you plan to do any type of social activities, you might want to advertise this right up front.

## WORSHIP
### *(15 Minutes – Optional for the First Meeting)*

Fifteen minutes is a solid time for a worship segment. That said, it all depends upon the culture of your group. If everyone is okay with doing 30 minutes of praise and worship, by all means, go for it!

For this particular curriculum, a worship segment is highly recommended, as true and lasting transformation happens as we continually encounter God's presence.

## PRAYER/MINISTRY TIME
### *(5–15 Minutes)*

At this point, you will transition from either welcome or worship into a time of prayer.

Just like praise and worship, it is recommended that this initial time of prayer be five to ten minutes in length; but if the group is made up of people who do not mind praying longer, it should not be discouraged. The key is stewarding everyone's time well while maintaining focus on the most important things at hand.

The prayer component is a time where group members will not just receive prayer, but also learn how to exercise Jesus' authority in their own lives and witness breakthrough in their circumstances.

After the door is opened through worship, the atmosphere is typically charged with God's Presence.

## TRANSITION TIME

At this point, you will transition from prayer/ministry time to watching the *Receiving Healing from the Courts of Heaven* DVDs.

**Group leaders/class teachers**: It is recommended that you have the DVD in the player and are all ready to press "play" on the appropriate session.

## VIDEO/TEACHING
*(20–25 Minutes)*

During this time, group members will answer the questions in their workbooks and have a place to take notes.

## SUMMARY

There is also short summary of the week's topic before the discussion questions. You can read this prior to the group meeting to provide you with a summary of that week's session.

## DISCUSSION QUESTIONS
*(20–30 minutes)*

In the Leader's Guide there will be a number of questions to ask the group. Some questions will be phrased so you can ask them directly, others may have instructions or suggestions for how you can guide the discussion.

Some lessons will have more questions than others. Also, there might be some instances where you choose to cut out certain questions for the sake of time. This is entirely up to you, and in a circumstance where the Holy Spirit is moving and appears to be highlighting some questions more than others, flow in sync with the Holy Spirit. He will not steer you wrong!

As you ask the question in the group setting, encourage more than one person to provide an answer. Usually, you will have some people who are way off in their responses, but you will also have those who provide *part* of the correct answer.

Participants may feel like the conversation was lively, the dialogue insightful, and that the meeting was an overall success; but when all is said and done, the question, *"What do I do next?"* is not sufficiently answered. This is why every discussion time will be followed with an activation segment.

## ACTIVATION
### (5–10 Minutes)

- Each activation segment should be five to ten minutes at the *minimum*, as this is the place where believers begin putting into action what they just learned.

- The activation segment will be custom-tailored for the session covered.

- Even though every group member might not be able to participate in the activation exercise, it gives them a visual for what it looks like to demonstrate the concept that they just studied.

## PLANS FOR THE NEXT WEEK
### (2 Minutes)

Be sure to let group members know if the meeting location will change or differ from week to week, or if there are any other relevant announcements to your group/class. Weekly e-mails, Facebook updates, and text messages are great tools to communicate with your group. If your church has a database tool that allows for communication between small group/class leaders and members, that is an effective avenue for interaction as well.

## CLOSE IN PRAYER

This is a good opportunity to ask for a volunteer to conclude the meeting with prayer.

# Week 1

# HEALING IN THE HEAVENS

It's God's will that His children live in health and abundance. Jesus died to free us from sickness, making suffering illegal. So why do we sometimes experience pain and illness on this side of the cross? Though Jesus accomplished everything needed to undo this curse, Satan often strategically brings legal cases against us. In response, God invites us to the Courts of Heaven where He not only reverses the legal accusations of the enemy but leads us into the abundance Jesus secured for us.

# JOURNAL NOTES

## Week 1

# VIDEO LISTENING GUIDE

1. Acts 10:38 says "Jesus went about doing good and healing all those who were **oppressed** by the **devil**."

2. Jesus commissions us to carry the same **anointing** and **power** that He carried.

3. As we see in scripture, before Jesus releases His **healing**, He deals with **legal** issues.

4. First Peter 5:8 calls the devil our "adversary." The word "adversary" means "one who brings a **lawsuit**."

5. If we feel the enemy may be hindering us, we need to identify if he is working **legal**ly or **illegal**ly in our lives.

   **Prayer Focus**: Ask the Lord to help every participant 1) understand why it's so important to fight the enemy's schemes when seeking healing and 2) have continual hope in the work Jesus has done on the cross.

## SUMMARY

In this week's lesson, Robert introduces the concept of the Courts of Heaven. When we understand how the enemy works against us, we can pursue healing and freedom from bondage. As we see throughout scripture, He gives us the tools we need to overcome the work of the enemy so we can live free and whole. Are you ready to gain new tools for fully experiencing the freedom and health Jesus died for you to have?

## God's Heart for Healing

Jesus intends for all of His people to live healed, free from sickness and disease. But before we can step into the healing God has for us in Jesus, we must first recognize the ways the enemy resists healing in our lives so we can deal with them first.

Though Jesus set everything in place for us to be healed, Satan can work against us legally, bringing cases against us in supernatural courts. He can use our sin, unforgiveness, or even others' sin against us to keep us in bondage. That's why so many times in scripture, Jesus *forgave* people before He released His healing touch.

# PREPARE

## Reflect

Review the following key concepts from Robert's teaching this week to prepare your heart and mind to lead. Take some time to journal through the ideas that stick out to you.

- Jesus was the greatest philanthropist of all time, giving His wealth to bring healing to us.
- We are commissioned by Jesus to carry the same power He carried.
- To be "loosed" by God literally means to be legally set free from a claim against us.
- The enemy is our accuser, bringing claims against us—some are legitimate, and some are not.
- If we want to experience the anointing touch of the Lord, we first need to be freed from the legal claims the enemy has against us.

## Pause

Listen to God's heart for this week. Spend time in prayer asking the Lord what He wants to share with those in your group. Journal what you receive from Him. Make sure to include any ideas you have for your group time.

## FELLOWSHIP, WELCOME, AND INTRODUCTIONS
*(20-30 Minutes – For the First Meeting)*

**Welcome** everyone as they walk in. If it is a small group environment, as the host or leader, be intentional about connecting with each person as they come to the meeting space. If it is a church class environment, it is still recommended that the leader connects with each participant. However, there will be less pressure for the participants to feel connected immediately in a traditional class setting versus a more intimate small group environment.

In the small group, serve refreshments and facilitate fellowship between group members. In a class setting, talk with the attendees and ensure that they receive all of their necessary materials (the workbook and a copy of *Receiving Healing from the Courts of Heaven*).

**Introduce yourself** and allow participants to briefly introduce themselves as well. In a classroom setting, establish some type of flow and then have each person give a quick introduction (name, interesting fact, etc.).

**Discuss the schedule** for the meetings. Provide participants an overview of what the next eight weeks will look like and any potential social activities.

**Distribute materials** to each participant. Briefly orient the participants to the book and workbook, explaining the 15–20 minute time commitment for each day. Encourage each person to engage fully in this journey—they will get out of it only as much as they invest. This is a way to cultivate a habit of Bible study and daily time pursuing God's Presence, starting with just 15–20 minutes. Morning, evening, afternoon—*when* does not matter.

## OPENING PRAYER

## WORSHIP
*(15 Minutes – Optional for First Meeting)*

If a group chooses to do a worship segment, often they decide to begin on the second week. It usually takes an introductory meeting for everyone to become acquainted with one another and comfortable with their surroundings before they open up in worship.

## PRAYER/MINISTRY TIME
*(5–15 Minutes)*

# VIDEO/TEACHING
*(20 Minutes)*

# DISCUSSION QUESTIONS
*(25–30 Minutes)*

Spend some time dialoguing about the video content, covering the key concepts and talking points you prepared. Here are some possible questions you could use:

- What are some scriptural examples of God dealing with legal issues before bringing healing to someone?

- What does it mean to be "loosed" by God?

- When we are "loosed," what are we set free FROM and set free TO?

- How does understanding how the enemy works against us affect how we live?

Write down any questions that God puts on your heart.

_____
_____
_____
_____
_____
_____
_____
_____
_____
_____
_____

What does it mean to live truly "loosed" by the Lord?

_____
_____
_____
_____
_____
_____
_____
_____
_____
_____

## ACTIVATION: MEDITATE ON GOD'S HEART FOR YOUR HEALING

Take time individually to think about a time in your life you experienced physical healing. How did the Lord deal with your heart first before physical healing took place?

How did He free you from emotional/spiritual AND physical bondage in the process?

Spend time journaling about God's heart to give you freedom as a whole person and what it says about His heart for you.

Have a couple of members share about process God took them on to find healing. Have them pray for the same grace to be released on the group.

## CLOSE IN PRAYER

*Thank you for leading a group in Receiving Healing from the Courts of Heaven. We can't wait to see what the Lord does next week.*

# Week 2

# THE LEGAL BASIS FOR HEALING

Do you know the power of the blood of Jesus? Just like the blood of the sacrificial lamb on the Passover, Jesus' blood is our healing power, allowing us to be free from sickness. It allows us to escape judgment and to live free from the curse of sin. It's our role as His children to step into this gift, agreeing with the work He has done for us. This means when the enemy builds a case against us to keep us from healing, we can respond in faith!

# JOURNAL NOTES

## Week 2

# VIDEO LISTENING GUIDE

1. The legal basis of healing is the **atoning work** of Jesus on the **Cross**.

2. Jesus made sickness **illegal** when He died on the cross.

3. The Bible says Jesus "carried our sorrows" (Isaiah 53:4). The word "sorrow" literally means **pain**.

4. Faith is not a **quiet believing**. It is a **violent pursuit**.

5. Galatians 3:13 tells us Jesus became a **curse** for us. This means we no longer live under the **curse**.

**Prayer Focus**: Ask the Lord to help every participant 1) understand the work Jesus did on the cross to free us from suffering and 2) trust Him for freedom from sickness, sin, and death.

## SUMMARY

In this week's lesson, we learn about the legal basis for healing. When Jesus died on the cross, He accomplished everything necessary to bring us freedom from sickness and disease. He even intercedes for us in Heaven! It's our job to live in agreement with what Heaven says about us. However, sometimes the enemy can intervene and bring cases against us. This is why Robert calls faith a "violent pursuit."

## *The Power of Jesus' Blood*

Throughout scripture, we see examples of the power of a blood sacrifice. In the Old Testament, for example, the Israelites were protected by God when they marked their doors with the blood of a sacrificed lamb during the Passover. Similarly, when Jesus died, He became a literal blood sacrifice for us, that we might be free from the threat of the enemy for all time. However, we must come into agreement with what He's done for us before we experience it in fullness.

# PREPARE

## *Reflect*

Review the following key concepts from Robert's teaching this week to prepare your heart and mind to lead. Take some time to journal through the ideas that stick out to you.

- If we aren't firmly established in the legal basis from which God heals us, it is really difficult for us to have the faith we need to receive healing.

- When Jesus died on the cross, He made sickness and disease illegal.

- Many times, we tolerate things Jesus died for us to be free from.

- Though Jesus finished His work on the cross, we are called to appropriate and take hold of that which is ours in Him.

## *Pause*

Listen to God's heart for this week. Spend time in prayer asking the Lord what He wants to share with those in your group. Journal what you receive from Him. Make sure to include any ideas you have for your group time.

_____
_____
_____
_____
_____
_____
_____
_____
_____

# FELLOWSHIP, WELCOME, AND INTRODUCTIONS
*(20-30 Minutes — For the First Meeting)*

**Welcome everyone** as they walk in. Be sure to identify any new members who were not at the previous session, and be sure that they receive the appropriate materials—workbook and book.

**Encourage everyone to congregate** in the meeting place. If it is a classroom setting, make an announcement that it is time to sit down and begin the session. If it is a small group, ensure everyone makes their way to the designated meeting space.

# OPENING PRAYER

# WORSHIP
*(15-20 Minutes)*

## PRAYER/MINISTRY TIME
*(5–15 Minutes)*

## VIDEO/TEACHING
*(20 Minutes)*

## DISCUSSION QUESTIONS
*(25–30 Minutes)*

Spend some time dialoguing about the video content, covering the key concepts and talking points you prepared. Here are some possible questions you could use:

- What does it mean that we have a "legal basis" for healing?
- Why does the enemy get to intervene in our healing when Jesus gave us the means to be healed?
- What was the significance of the Passover in Exodus, and how does it relate to Jesus' work on the cross?
- What are the implications of Jesus becoming a curse for us?

Write down any questions that God puts on your heart.

We must come into agreement with what Jesus has done for us before we experience it in fullness.

## ACTIVATION: CLAIMING YOUR IDENTITY IN JESUS.

If possible, have praise and worship music ready to go—either live, or on some kind of audio system.

Declaring the truth when the enemy makes a case against you is a powerful way to reclaim your inheritance in God.

Take time to write out three to four declarations you can speak over yourself when you are coming against the enemy while seeking healing. Think about who God is, who He made you to be, and His heart for your healing and freedom. Hold on to these declarations and use them in your violent pursuit of what Jesus died for you to have!

Have members share their declarations with the group. After everyone has shared, pray over the group to have a new grace to walk out these declarations in their lives.

## CLOSE IN PRAYER

*Great work! Now let's move on to week 3 together, where we will learn more about the currency of Heaven.*

# Week 3

# UNDOING TRADES

When Jesus died on the cross, He traded His perfect life for our sin. In the same way, the enemy wants us to trade his lies for our freedom. While giving to God always results in increase for us, partnership with the devil's schemes opens us up to deeper pain and suffering. By God's power, we can undo the trades we've made with the evil one and move forward in the healing we were made for.

# JOURNAL NOTES

# Week 3

# VIDEO LISTENING GUIDE

1. Satan **hates** us because God gave us seats in the place he used to **occupy**.

2. The **Cross** of Jesus was the greatest trade that ever took place.

3. Every offering carries a **testimony** with it.

4. Bringing an offering is making a **trade** in the **spiritual** realm.

5. Trading with the enemy gives him **rights** he shouldn't have.

**Prayer Focus**: Ask the Lord to help every participant 1) to become aware of how they may have traded in their inheritance in any way and 2) boldly reclaim what is theirs in Jesus.

## SUMMARY

In this week's lesson, Robert introduces trades and how the wrong type of "trading" can keep us from experiencing healing. In scripture, every offering is a trade. When we bring sacrifices and offerings to God, He brings us increase. However, when we participate in trades with the enemy, we essentially give him the right to take from us what is ours. For this reason, it's essential that we draw near to the Lord in faith, giving ourselves, our time, and our hearts to Him alone.

### *The Ultimate Trade*

The cross of Jesus is the ultimate example of how trades work. When He died on the cross, He exchanged our sin and death for forgiveness and life. Because we believe in Him, we have access to this abundance of life. Now, as children of God, we can choose to participate in exchanges and trades with Him, or with the enemy. Both have their own consequences.

# PREPARE

## *Reflect*

Review the following key concepts from Robert's teaching this week to prepare your heart and mind to lead. Take some time to journal through the ideas that stick out to you.

- Satan hates us because God gave us a place he used to occupy.

- Since he can't create, Satan must copy, and that's why he tries to steal from us what is ours.

- The cross of Jesus was the greatest trade of all time because it traded our sin for His righteousness.

- All of our offerings have a testimony attached to them.

- God wants our offerings to come with the sound of love and devotion.

## *Pause*

Listen to God's heart for this week. Spend time in prayer asking the Lord what He wants to share with those in your group. Journal what you receive from Him. Make sure to include any ideas you have for your group time.

_____
_____
_____
_____
_____
_____
_____
_____
_____
_____

# FELLOWSHIP, WELCOME, AND INTRODUCTIONS

**Welcome everyone** as they walk in. Be sure to identify any new members who were not at the previous session, and be sure that they receive the appropriate materials—workbook and book.

**Encourage everyone to congregate** in the meeting place. If it is a classroom setting, make an announcement that it is time to sit down and begin the session. If it is a small group, ensure everyone makes their way to the designated meeting space.

# OPENING PRAYER

# WORSHIP
*(15-20 Minutes)*

# PRAYER/MINISTRY TIME
*(5–15 Minutes)*

# VIDEO/TEACHING
*(20 Minutes)*

# DISCUSSION QUESTIONS (25–30 MINUTES)

Spend some time dialoguing about the video content, covering the key concepts and talking points you prepared. Here are some possible questions you could use:

- What does it mean to trade with the enemy?
- What does it mean that our offering has a testimony attached to it?
- What do we get when we make an exchange or trade with the Lord?
- What are some common ways the devil tries to bring us on the trading floor with him?
- Why is it so important to resist trading with the enemy?

Write down any questions that God puts on your heart.

_____

_____

_____

_____

The cross of Jesus is the ultimate example of how trades work. When He died on the cross, He exchanged our sin and death for forgiveness and life.

## ACTIVATION: REVERSING TRADES

This will be an group *exercise*.

- Get into groups of two or three and spend some time sharing about how trading with the enemy in the past has affected you, as you are comfortable.

- What did you take from him, and what did he take from you?

- After sharing, pray out loud for one another to give the enemy back what you never wanted, and ask the Lord in Jesus' name to restore all He has for you instead.

After you have prayed, have a time of praise and worship. This is a time to offer up thanksgiving to God for all that He restores!

## CLOSE IN PRAYER

*You're doing a great job leading your group. Are you ready for next week as we learn about the covenants we can create in trades?*

## Week 4

# THE COVENANT IN TRADES

Did you know the enemy can't create like God can? He can only copy. In order to build his kingdom of darkness, he must convince us to work alongside him. When we participate in trades with the enemy, he uses what we give him to build his kingdom of darkness. Only when we undo our trades and revoke covenants we've made with him will we be free to live in health and wholeness.

# JOURNAL NOTES

# Week 4

# VIDEO LISTENING GUIDE

1. The enemy can't **create** anything; He can only **copy**.

2. Our **agreements** help the enemy build his **kingdom**.

3. The purpose of **trades** is to create **covenants**.

4. God calls us to go to the Courts of **Heaven** and reclaim what **belongs** to us.

5. Isaiah 28:15 tells us the danger of making a **covenant** with **Satan**.

**Prayer Focus**: Ask the Lord to help every participant 1) recognize how covenants with the enemy can keep them from healing and 2) renounce every covenant they've made outside the Lord so they can live in abundance and freedom.

## SUMMARY

This week, we discovered the danger of making covenants with the enemy, and how covenants and trades are related. When we trade with Satan, we enter into an agreement with him, which can position us under his power. When we revoke this covenant in the Courts of Heaven and restore ourselves to God, we can regain the inheritance we were always meant to have in Him.

## *The Power of Covenants*

Scripture is full of covenants. A binding agreement between two parties, a covenant is basically a lifelong promise that can keep us bound to the person or power we come into contract with. Trading with the enemy gives him power in our lives because when we participate with his schemes, we enter into a binding contract with him. Who will we choose to be in relationship with, the Lord or the enemy?

# PREPARE

## *Reflect*

Review the following key concepts from Robert's teaching this week to prepare your heart and mind to lead. Take some time to journal through the ideas that stick out to you.

- Satan wants us to trade with him so he can take what belongs to us to build his own kingdom.

- The whole purpose of the enemy's trades is to create covenants.

- Trades give the enemy legal right to claim ownership over us, which creates arguments in the spirit realm.

- When we go to the Courts of Heaven, God calls us to both annul our covenants with darkness and to give back whatever we may have gained from those covenants.

## *Pause*

Listen to God's heart for this week. Spend time in prayer asking the Lord what He wants to share with those in your group. Journal what you receive from Him. Make sure to include any ideas you have for your group time.

## FELLOWSHIP, WELCOME, AND INTRODUCTIONS

**Welcome everyone** as they walk in. Be sure to identify any new members who were not at the previous session, and be sure that they receive the appropriate materials—workbook and book.

**Encourage everyone to congregate** in the meeting place. If it is a classroom setting, make an announcement that it is time to sit down and begin the session. If it is a small group, ensure everyone makes their way to the designated meeting space.

## OPENING PRAYER

## WORSHIP
*(15-20 Minutes)*

# PRAYER/MINISTRY TIME
*(5–15 Minutes)*

# VIDEO/TEACHING
*(20 Minutes)*

# DISCUSSION QUESTIONS
*(25–30 Minutes)*

Spend some time dialoguing about the video content, covering the key concepts and talking points you prepared. Here are some possible questions you could use:

- How are trades and covenants connected?
- What are some examples of covenants in scripture?
- What were the outcomes of these covenants?
- How can we renounce old covenants in the Courts of Heaven?
- What does it mean to be in covenant with the Lord?

Write down any questions that God puts on your heart.

Trading with the enemy gives him power over our lives because when we participate with his schemes, we enter into a binding contract with him. Will we choose to be bound to the Lord or to the enemy?

## ACTIVATION: DIVORCING THE ENEMY

Breaking a covenant with the enemy is like a divorce. Take some time to journal about all the implications of "divorcing" the enemy.

This will be a group *exercise*. Have the group break into groups of two or three. Pray for groups to have the spirit of widom and revelation to recognize areas where they have knowingly or unknowingly created covenants with the enemy.

Have the member share what would it look like to break covenant with the enemy? Think about earthly divorce. What are all the steps, implications, and outcomes of divorcing Satan?

Then have the members pray for each other to walk out their breakthrough and freedom.

## CLOSE IN PRAYER

*God is doing a powerful work! Thank you for all your time and leadership. Let's move on to the next lesson together.*

## Week 5

# DEALING WITH DEDICATIONS

More than just afflicting us individually, the enemy can stake his claim over entire bloodlines. Dedications, which are the result of trades and covenants made with Satan, enable him to work against us and steal from us. By breaking ties with the enemy and his schemes in the Courts of Heaven, we can be free from the dedications we have knowingly or unknowingly made to him. God invites us to come under the Lordship of Christ instead, submitting to His Lordship alone!

# JOURNAL NOTES

# Week 5

# Video Listening Guide

1. Dedications are the enemy declaring that he **owns** you and your **bloodline**.

2. When we are born again, we move from the kingdom of **darkness** to the kingdom of **light**. But this doesn't mean the devil automatically gives up his **rights**.

3. Covenants in our **bloodline** can dedicate us to a dark **power**, but Jesus' blood can free us from it.

4. Jesus is not just our **savior**, but our **Lord**.

5. Coming under Jesus' **Lordship** means no other **power** has the right to claim us.

**Prayer Focus**: Ask the Lord to help every participant 1) see dedications that may have taken place in their bloodline and 2) trust in the Lord to bring freedom and light where there is bondage darkness.

## SUMMARY

In this week's lesson, we learn about how dedications can affect our lives. As a result of the covenants we've made with the enemy, knowingly or unknowingly, we give him ownership over us and our bloodline. Similarly, we can still be affected today by dedications that took place generations ago. Jesus' blood shed on the cross is the only power that can free us from these dedications, and He invites us to come under His Lordship so we might be free.

## *The Power of Dedications*

Dedications are like the next level of agreements made with the enemy. What starts with a trade evolves into a covenant which then becomes a dedication, or a "devotion" of an individual or bloodline to him, which essentially gives him ownership over those things.

# PREPARE

## *Reflect*

Review the following key concepts from Robert's teaching this week to prepare your heart and mind to lead. Take some time to journal through the ideas that stick out to you.

- Dedications are the enemy declaring that he now owns you and your bloodline based on a covenant.

- He, as a result, tries to not only work things against you but for generations to come.

- Just because Jesus gave us new life doesn't mean the devil gives up his rights automatically.

- Coming under the Lordship of Jesus means no other power has a right to claim us.

## *Pause*

Listen to God's heart for this week. Spend time in prayer asking the Lord what He wants to share with those in your group. Journal what you receive from Him. Make sure to include any ideas you have for your group time.

## FELLOWSHIP, WELCOME, AND INTRODUCTIONS

**Welcome everyone** as they walk in. Be sure to identify any new members who were not at the previous session, and be sure that they receive the appropriate materials—workbook and book.

**Encourage everyone to congregate** in the meeting place. If it is a classroom setting, make an announcement that it is time to sit down and begin the session. If it is a small group, ensure everyone makes their way to the designated meeting space.

## OPENING PRAYER

# WORSHIP
*(15-20 Minutes)*

# PRAYER/MINISTRY TIME
*(5-15 Minutes)*

# VIDEO/TEACHING
*(20 Minutes)*

# DISCUSSION QUESTIONS
*(25-30 Minutes)*

Spend some time dialoguing about the video content, covering the key concepts and talking points you prepared. Here are some possible questions you could use:

- Beyond his attacks on us individually, how can the enemy affect our bloodline?

- How does being born again affect our identity and our place in the spiritual realm?

- Why does the enemy still get to make claims against us even though Jesus died for our sins?

- What removes the power of dedications from our lives?

- Why is it so important that we submit to Jesus as Lord, not just worship Him as Savior?

Write down any questions that God puts on your heart.

_____
_____
_____
_____
_____
_____

When Jesus died on the cross, He saved us from the power of both sin and death, eradicating the power of disease and sickness over us. That's why we call Him our Savior. However, He is much more than that.

## ACTIVATION: SUBMITTING OURSELVES TO THE LORDSHIP OF JESUS

Removing dedications isn't just about saying "no" to the enemy. It's about saying "yes" to Jesus and submitting to His Lordship over our lives. There are many ways we can live under His Lordship, and one is to dedicate ourselves to Him.

This will be an individual *exercise*. Take some time to journal and write a letter of dedication to the Lord, renouncing any old agreements you may have with the enemy. List out any areas of your life you want to renew your dedication to Him.

Have a couple of the participants read their letters to the group. Then have a time of praise and worship. This is a time to offer up thanksgiving to God for all that He restores!

## CLOSE IN PRAYER

*God will honor the work you are doing to lead your group! We are praying for you as you move on to week 6.*

# Week 6

# The Power of Unforgiveness

In the Courts of Heaven, forgiveness is a powerful currency. Just as the Lord has fully forgiven us in Jesus, we must forgive those who have hurt or sinned against us. If we choose to hold someone in judgment and allow a root of bitterness to spring up, we give the enemy power to steal from us. Instead, we can step into forgiveness, offering grace to others just as God has done for us.

# JOURNAL NOTES

# Week 6

# VIDEO LISTENING GUIDE

1. In the Lord's prayer, we pray that we'd **forgive** others as they **trespass** against us.

2. God leaves us no room to carry **bitterness** and **anger** in our hearts.

3. Forgiveness is releasing someone else from **judgment**.

4. We don't forgive others in our own **power**. We simply **extend** what God has given to us.

5. James 5:13 shows us that **forgiveness** is directly connected to **healing**.

   **Prayer Focus**: Ask the Lord to help every participant 1) understand the significance of being forgiven by God and 2) forgive others who have trespassed against them.

## SUMMARY

In lesson 6, we discover the importance of forgiveness and how it is connected to our physical healing. Before God releases us into the healing we long for, He often wants to deal with our hearts and release us from emotional bondage. That's why it's so important that we practice forgiveness. As God forgave us when we came to Jesus, we are called to forgive those who have wronged us.

### *God's Heart for Forgiveness*

Forgiveness is a major priority to God. We see it throughout scripture. Even as the Israelites continued to make offerings to idols, God displayed His mercy to them. He continues to show His grace and mercy to His children today. Without experiencing His forgiveness and forgiving others, we can't walk in the abundance of what God has for us, which includes our healing.

# PREPARE

## *Reflect*

Review the following key concepts from Robert's teaching this week to prepare your heart and mind to lead. Take some time to journal through the ideas that stick out to you.

- God leaves no room to carry bitterness and anger in our hearts.

- Carrying bitterness and unforgiveness can affect us spiritually, emotionally, and physically.

- When God says He is releasing forgiveness and mercy; and we won't give it to someone else, that's a great insult to Him.

- We don't forgive out of our own power. We extend what He's given to us.

- If I refuse to forgive, I am cutting myself off from the grace that brings both forgiveness and healing.

## Pause

Listen to God's heart for this week. Spend time in prayer asking the Lord what He wants to share with those in your group. Journal what you receive from Him. Make sure to include any ideas you have for your group time.

_____
_____
_____
_____
_____
_____
_____
_____

# FELLOWSHIP, WELCOME, AND INTRODUCTIONS

**Welcome everyone** as they walk in. Be sure to identify any new members who were not at the previous session, and be sure that they receive the appropriate materials—workbook and book.

**Encourage everyone to congregate** in the meeting place. If it is a classroom setting, make an announcement that it is time to sit down and begin the session. If it is a small group, ensure everyone makes their way to the designated meeting space.

# OPENING PRAYER

# WORSHIP
*(15-20 Minutes)*

# PRAYER/MINISTRY TIME
*(5–15 Minutes)*

# VIDEO/TEACHING
*(20 Minutes)*

# DISCUSSION QUESTIONS
*(25–30 Minutes)*

Spend some time dialoguing about the video content, covering the key concepts and talking points you prepared. Here are some possible questions you could use:

- How are forgiveness and healing related?
- What does James 5 teach us about the grace of forgiveness and healing?
- How can a root of bitterness affect our lives?
- Why does our unforgiveness offend God?
- What is the best way to move forward when we don't *feel* like forgiving someone?

Write down any questions that God puts on your heart.

Spiritual, emotional, and physical healing go hand in hand.

## ACTIVATION: EXAMINING OUR HEARTS FOR UNFORGIVENESS

Spend some time with the Lord and ask Him to reveal anyone in your life you have not forgiven. Who do you have anger or bitterness toward?

Write out a prayer of forgiveness over this person, releasing this person from your judgment.

If you are struggling, ask God to help you by showing you the power of the forgiveness He has extended to you through Jesus.

Have the participants get in groups of two or three and share with the group who they are needing to forgive. Have them minister and pray for each other to walk in new levels of courage and forgiveness to release people from the bondage of unforgiveness.

## CLOSE IN PRAYER

*Onto the last week! Can you believe we're almost there? God will give you grace to finish strong!*

# Week 7

# UNDOING WORD CURSES

The power of life and death are in the tongue. When those in authority speak words of criticism or judgment over us, they become expert witnesses in Satan's trial against us. Only by agreeing with the identity God has given us as His beloved children will we gain us victory against the enemy's schemes. When we repent for our own curses, forgive those who have cursed us, and break off the power of words spoken against us, we will experience the freedom and wholeness we long for.

# JOURNAL NOTES

# Week 7

# VIDEO LISTENING GUIDE

1. We can experience **physical issues** because people spoke **evil**, **critical**, or **curse** words over us.

2. People with **authority** over us are particularly damaging to us in the spirit realm.

3. The **word** of Joshua became a **curse** over the city of Jericho.

4. Isaiah 54:17 says that "no **weapon** formed against you shall prosper, and every tongue which rises against you in judgment you shall **condemn**."

5. "Tongue [word] which rises in judgment" literally means a **verdict rendered**.

**Prayer Focus**: Ask the Lord to help every participant 1) grasp the power of words to bring life and death and 2) be free from the curses others have spoken over their lives.

## SUMMARY

In our final lesson, Robert shows us the significance of curses and how we can undo them in the Spirit. While curses spoken over us can block the flow of Jesus' healing, we have power in Him to break them off and take hold of all He has for us.

## *The Power of Curses*

Whether someone spoke something over our family line decades ago or a loved one said something critical just yesterday, words can be damaging weapons against us, holding us back from the healing Jesus intends to show us. Critical or judgmental words others speak allow the enemy to build a case against us, and it's our job to cast off these words and walk in the truth of who He is and who we are in Him.

# PREPARE

## *Reflect*

Review the following key concepts from Robert's teaching this week to prepare your heart and mind to lead. Take some time to journal through the ideas that stick out to you.

- Those in authority over us have unique power to speak curses over our lives.
- The enemy takes those words from people and uses them to build cases against us in the spirit realm.
- These curses, often judgmental or critical words, can form a sentence over our lives.
- They can affect us emotionally and spiritually, but also physically.
- It is our right as children of God that no weapon formed against us will remain and no word spoken over us in judgment will stand (see Isaiah 54:17).

## *Pause*

Listen to God's heart for this week. Spend time in prayer asking the Lord what He wants to share with those in your group. Journal what you receive from Him. Make sure to include any ideas you have for your group time.

_____
_____
_____
_____
_____
_____
_____
_____
_____
_____

# FELLOWSHIP, WELCOME, AND INTRODUCTIONS

**Welcome everyone** as they walk in.

**Encourage everyone to congregate** in the meeting place. If it is a classroom setting, make an announcement that it is time to sit down and begin the session. If it is a small group, ensure everyone makes their way to the designated meeting space.

# OPENING PRAYER

# WORSHIP
*(15-20 Minutes)*

# PRAYER/MINISTRY TIME
*(5–15 Minutes)*

# VIDEO/TEACHING
*(20 Minutes)*

# DISCUSSION QUESTIONS
*(25–30 Minutes)*

Spend some time dialoguing about the video content, covering the key concepts and talking points you prepared. Here are some possible questions you could use:

- How and why do curses spoken over us by people in authority have special weight in the spiritual realm?

- How did Joshua's curse affect Jericho?

- Why do we need to forgive those who have cursed us?

- What does it mean to "annul" curses spoken over us?

- What does God replace our curses with when we repent, renounce lies, and seek restoration to Him?

Write down any questions that God puts on your heart.

Because curses and the corresponding work of the enemy in our lives can hold us in sickness, it's crucial that we work with the Spirit to undo the curses that are affecting our lives.

## ACTIVATION: PRAYING OVER OUR DESTINY

Gather in small groups of two and take time to pray over one another. Ask the Lord for prophetic insights on one another's destiny, and pray that He would release each other into the great purpose He designed.

Thank Him for His plan for your life and all that He's done to secure abundant life on your behalf!

Have each of the participants share one thing that deeply impacted them from your seven weeks together.

Then have a time of praise and worship. This is a time to offer up thanksgiving to God for what He has done for them through these seven weeks together.

## CLOSE IN PRAYER

*Thank you so much for your time, effort, and dedication for the last seven weeks. We pray God did a great work in your heart as you led your group to greater freedom.*

# ABOUT ROBERT HENDERSON

Robert Henderson is a global apostolic leader who operates in revelation and impartation. His teaching empowers the body of Christ to see the hidden truths of Scripture clearly and apply them for breakthrough results. Driven by a mandate to disciple nations through writing and speaking, Robert travels extensively around the globe, teaching on the apostolic, the Kingdom of God, the "Seven Mountains," and, most notably, the Courts of Heaven. He has been married to Mary for forty years. They have six children and five grandchildren. Together they are enjoying life in beautiful Midlothian, Texas.

## *Looking for more from Robert Henderson?*

*Purchase* additional resources—CDs, DVDs, digital downloads, music—from Robert Henderson at www.roberthenderson.org/store.

Visit www.roberthenderson.org
for more information on Robert Henderson,
to view their speaking itinerary,
or to look into additional teaching resources.

# INCREASE THE EFFECTIVENESS OF YOUR PRAYERS.

## Learn how to release your destiny from Heaven's Courts!

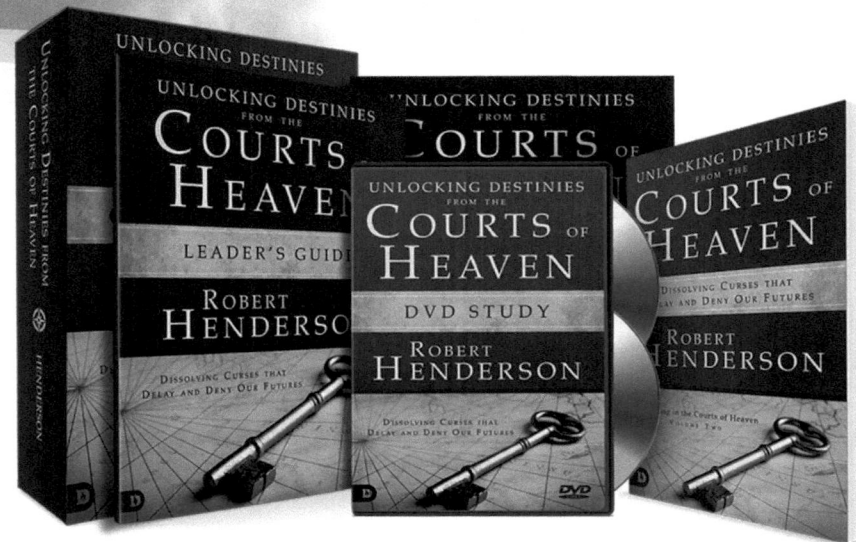

**Unlocking Destinies from the Courts of Heaven**
*Curriculum Box Set Includes:*
9 Video Teaching Sessions (2 DVD Disks), Unlocking Destinies *book*,
Interactive Manual, Leader's Guide

There are books in Heaven that record your destiny and purpose. Their pages describe the very reason you were placed on the Earth.

And yet, there is a war against your destiny being fulfilled. Your archenemy, the devil, knows that as you occupy your divine assignment, by default, the powers of darkness are demolished. Heaven comes to Earth as God's people fulfill their Kingdom callings!

In the *Unlocking Destinies from the Courts of Heaven* book and curriculum, Robert Henderson takes you step by step through a prophetic prayer strategy. By watching the powerful video sessions and going through the Courts of Heaven process using the interactive manual, you will learn how to dissolve the delays and hindrances to your destiny being fulfilled.

# FREE E-BOOKS? YES, PLEASE!

Get **FREE** and deeply-discounted **Christian books** for your **e-reader** delivered to your inbox **every week!**

## IT'S SIMPLE!

**VISIT** lovetoreadclub.com

**SUBSCRIBE** by entering your email address

**RECEIVE** free and discounted e-book offers and inspiring articles delivered to your inbox every week!

Unsubscribe at any time.

## SUBSCRIBE NOW!

LOVE TO READ CLUB

visit **LOVETOREADCLUB.COM** ▶

Printed by Libri Plureos GmbH in Hamburg, Germany